Acting Edition

Rez Politics and The Council

by William S. Yellow Robe, Jr.

‖SAMUEL FRENCH‖

Rez Politics Copyright © 1991 by William S. Yellow Robe, Jr.
The Council Copyright © 1991 (Rev. 2007) by William S. Yellow Robe, Jr.
All Rights Reserved

REZ POLITICS and *THE COUNCIL* are fully protected under the copyright laws of the United States of America, the British Commonwealth, including Canada, and all member countries of the Berne Convention for the Protection of Literary and Artistic Works, the Universal Copyright Convention, and/or the World Trade Organization conforming to the Agreement on Trade Related Aspects of Intellectual Property Rights. All rights, including professional and amateur stage productions, recitation, lecturing, public reading, motion picture, radio broadcasting, television, online/digital production, and the rights of translation into foreign languages are strictly reserved.

ISBN 978-0-573-71052-0

www.concordtheatricals.com
www.concordtheatricals.co.uk

FOR PRODUCTION INQUIRIES
UNITED STATES AND CANADA
info@concordtheatricals.com
1-866-979-0447

UNITED KINGDOM AND EUROPE
licensing@concordtheatricals.co.uk
020-7054-7298

Each title is subject to availability from Concord Theatricals Corp., depending upon country of performance. Please be aware that *REZ POLITICS* and *THE COUNCIL* may not be licensed by Concord Theatricals Corp. in your territory. Professional and amateur producers should contact the nearest Concord Theatricals Corp. office or licensing partner to verify availability.

CAUTION: Professional and amateur producers are hereby warned that *REZ POLITICS* and *THE COUNCIL* are subject to a licensing fee. The purchase, renting, lending or use of this book does not constitute a license to perform this title(s), which license must be obtained from Concord Theatricals Corp. prior to any performance. Performance of this title(s) without a license is a violation of federal law and may subject the producer and/or presenter of such performances to civil penalties. Both amateurs and professionals considering a production are strongly advised to apply to the appropriate agent before starting rehearsals, advertising, or booking a theatre. A licensing fee must be paid whether the title(s) is presented for charity or gain and whether or not admission is charged. Professional/Stock licensing fees are quoted upon application to Concord Theatricals Corp.

This work is published by Samuel French, an imprint of Concord Theatricals Corp.

No one shall make any changes in this title(s) for the purpose of production. No part of this book may be reproduced, stored in a retrieval system, scanned, uploaded, or transmitted in any form, by any means, now known or yet to be invented, including mechanical, electronic, digital, photocopying, recording, videotaping, or otherwise, without the prior written permission of the publisher. No one shall share this title(s), or any part of this title(s), through any social media or file hosting websites.

For all inquiries regarding motion picture, television, online/digital and other media rights, please contact Concord Theatricals Corp.

MUSIC AND THIRD-PARTY MATERIALS USE NOTE

Licensees are solely responsible for obtaining formal written permission from copyright owners to use copyrighted music and/or other copyrighted third-party materials (e.g. artworks, logos) in the performance of this play and are strongly cautioned to do so. If no such permission is obtained by the licensee, then the licensee must use only original music and materials that the licensee owns and controls. Licensees are solely responsible and liable for clearances of all third-party copyrighted materials, including without limitation music, and shall indemnify the copyright owners of the play(s) and their licensing agent, Concord Theatricals Corp., against any costs, expenses, losses and liabilities arising from the use of such copyrighted third-party materials by licensees. For music, please contact the appropriate music licensing authority in your territory for the rights to any incidental music.

IMPORTANT BILLING AND CREDIT REQUIREMENTS

If you have obtained performance rights to this title, please refer to your licensing agreement for important billing and credit requirements.

Dear Reader:

Please know that this play is published in its raw and unedited form. As such, you may notice elements that could be perceived as typographical or grammatical errors. You may also encounter what seem to be unfinished expressions.

Rather than altering the original work and speculating on Mr. Yellow Robe's authorial intent, we decided to present this play as we found it. We believe this decision best honors Mr. Yellow Robe's creative process and authorial intent while acknowledging that he did not have the opportunity to make final edits.

Should any questions arise as you read or perform this play, please contact us at info@thedgcm.org.

Thank you,
DG Copyright Management, Inc.

Rez Politics

REZ POLITICS first premiered at the University of Maine, Orono, ME, on February 5, at the Cyrus Pavilion Theater, and on February 23, at the University Club in the Fogler Library, as part of the Black Student Union celebration of Black History Month – 2009. The cast was as follows:

CURTIS .... Zachary Robbins
GERALD .... Nick Bear (Penobscot Tribe)

CHARACTERS

CURTIS – a large boy about ten
GERALD – smaller in size, about ten

SETTING

A field in Montana.

TIME

Early 1970s, afternoon.

(**CURTIS** *enters the acting area being chased by* **GERALD** *in a friendly game of tag. They enter the acting area with* **GERALD** *tagging* **CURTIS**. **GERALD** *enjoys his small victory.* **CURTIS** *looks around the area as if checking to see if they are noticed.* **CURTIS** *walks over to* **GERALD** *and gives him a hard shove.)*

CURTIS. My dad says you guys are nothing but a bunch of niggers.

GERALD. Yeah? But you guys aren't even Indian. You guys aren't even from here.

CURTIS. Yeah? So?

GERALD. Doesn't make you better than us.

CURTIS. You and your whole family are nothing but breeds.

GERALD. You too.

CURTIS. But we're more Indian than you guys are.

GERALD. No, you're not.

CURTIS. That's what my family said.

GERALD. They're wrong too.

CURTIS. So – you want to fight?

GERALD. I don't know.

CURTIS. Bet you can't fight.

(He begins to circle **GERALD**.*)*

GERALD. I'm not afraid of you.

CURTIS. I bet you are. Damn nigger.

GERALD. To hell with you, Curtis. I thought we were supposed to be friends.

CURTIS. I guess you thought wrong.

GERALD. Why are you doing this, anyway? I didn't do anything to you.

CURTIS. Yes you did.

GERALD. What then?

CURTIS. You know.

GERALD. No I don't.

> (**CURTIS** *has* **GERALD** *on the ground and circles him. He kicks at* **GERALD** *in the next few lines.*)

CURTIS. You're just trying to get out of this.

GERALD. Oww, you shit.

CURTIS. You know what you did.

GERALD. Oww!

CURTIS. Lying nigger.

GERALD. You shit head!

CURTIS. Get up, Gerald! Get up!

GERALD. Why did you hit me, you shit head!

CURTIS. Get up!

GERALD. You shit!

CURTIS. Come on. What are you going to do about it? Cry? Come on, Gerald, let's fight!

GERALD. All right, you ass!

> (**GERALD** *out-maneuvers* **CURTIS** *and gets to his feet and knocks* **CURTIS** *to the ground, getting the upper hand on* **CURTIS**.*)*

CURTIS. You piss head! Oww! Oww!

GERALD. You want to fight? Huh? Huh? Still want to fight? You damn breed!

CURTIS. Stop! I didn't hit you when you were down.

GERALD. Well, I'm not down.

CURTIS. Quit it!

GERALD. Are you going to cry? Huh?

CURTIS. Knock it off, you damn nigger!

GERALD. Stop calling me that!

CURTIS. Indins aren't supposed to be fighting each other.

GERALD. Oh – I'm an Indin now, huh?

CURTIS. I didn't say you weren't an Indian.

GERALD. Then why did you try to fight me than, huh?

CURTIS. Because – because I was told to.

GERALD. Who – who told you to fight me?

CURTIS. My brother, Gary. He told me I should kick your black ass.

GERALD. Piss on you, Curtis.

> (**GERALD** *threatens to strike* **CURTIS**, *making him flinch.*)

CURTIS. Oww! Stop it! Let me get up. You couldn't do this, if I could get up.

GERALD. No. You stay there. I won't let you up until you tell me why your brother Gary wants you to beat me up.

CURTIS. I already told you. He doesn't like you, your brother, or your sisters because you guys are part nigger.

GERALD. Well, I play around with you, and you're part white.

CURTIS. That isn't the same.

GERALD. Why?

CURTIS. We're part Indian and White.

GERALD. So?

CURTIS. You're part nigger.

GERALD. Yeah, but you guys aren't full bloods either.

CURTIS. I know.

GERALD. So why's Gary mad at me?

CURTIS. Because you guys are part nigger – colored.

GERALD. I didn't do anything to you.

CURTIS. I know.

GERALD. Gee, Curtis. I thought we were friends.

CURTIS. We were I guess.

GERALD. If your brother doesn't like me so much, why didn't he try to fight me after school today?

CURTIS. Because he's afraid of your older brother, Lewis.

GERALD. I should go and tell Lewis.

CURTIS. No! If you do, Lewis will beat up Gary, and then when Gary finds out, he'll beat me up.

GERALD. Why shouldn't I? We aren't friends.

CURTIS. Let me up – please, Gerald.

GERALD. Okay.

> (**CURTIS** *eases into a sitting position and* **GERALD** *slowly sits on the ground near him.*)

If you try anything, I'll beat you up again.

CURTIS. I won't do anything.

GERALD. All right.

CURTIS. Gerald, I – I didn't mean any of this.

GERALD. What do you mean?

CURTIS. I wasn't going to hurt you.

GERALD. Then why did you try to fight me?

CURTIS. I don't know.

GERALD. Gee, Curtis. Remember when Kenneth and his friends caught you by the water fountain yesterday and started hitting you? I was the one who stuck up for you.

CURTIS. Yeah, I remember.

GERALD. They were beating you up because you are a breed.

CURTIS. Yeah, I know.

GERALD. So why are you making fun of me and my family?

CURTIS. I don't know, Gerald. I guess I already told you.

GERALD. Yeah, but why?

CURTIS. I don't know. Maybe it's because my dad calls your dad "nigger" all the time?

GERALD. What?

CURTIS. Yeah. Whenever your dad comes over and when he leaves, my dad always says, "I'm glad that damn nigger Stan left."

GERALD. Really?

CURTIS. Yeah. And then he says, "We might not be full-blooded but at least we ain't part niggers like those Robes."

GERALD. Your dad says that?

CURTIS. All the time. What's wrong?

GERALD. We're not part nigger.

CURTIS. Yes you guys are.

GERALD. How would you know?

CURTIS. When Lewis used to grow his hair long, it was always curly. That's how everyone knows.

GERALD. Yeah, but your dad is bald.

CURTIS. That's because we're part white.

GERALD. And you guys aren't even from here.

CURTIS. What do you mean?

GERALD. We're Assiniboine. We're from here. You guys are Cree from South Dakota.

CURTIS. Yeah, but we're Indins.

GERALD. But not from here, and not this land.

CURTIS. Yeah, but still we're not – well, you know.

GERALD. Do you believe what your dad says?

CURTIS. Yeah. I guess I do. Sort of.

GERALD. I guess we shouldn't be around each other, huh?

CURTIS. I don't know.

GERALD. Should I come over to your house and get my bat?

CURTIS. I don't know.

GERALD. And you should come over and get your BB rifle.

CURTIS. And my army men?

GERALD. No. We left them at your house yesterday when we were playing at the hill.

CURTIS. Gerald? Are you mad?

GERALD. About what?

CURTIS. You know – what I did?

GERALD. I don't know. I'm mad at you, Gary, and your dad.

CURTIS. My father probably didn't mean it. He drinks a lot.

GERALD. Yeah, but what about Gary?

CURTIS. I wouldn't worry about him. I don't even like him. He's always hitting me.

GERALD. Yeah. Like that last time we stole his lighter to pop our firecrackers. He really got mad.

CURTIS. Yeah. Stupid shit.

GERALD. Did your dad ever give his lighter back to him?

CURTIS. No. He still has it.

(They share a laugh. Then awkwardness.)

Gerald? Do you – you know, get mad when other kids call you nigger? I know I would.

GERALD. Yeah. I do. I don't like it.

CURTIS. How did you – how did you guys get to be that way, you know?

GERALD. I don't know. I never asked my mom or my dad. How did you guys get to be part white?

CURTIS. My mom says it's because my dad is part white. What about you?

GERALD. I don't know.

CURTIS. Well, didn't your mom tell you it was because of your dad?

GERALD. No. My mom and dad never talk about things like that. At least I've never heard them. They're always laughing and teasing. I remember one time my dad came home mad one time.

CURTIS. Yeah? Why?

GERALD. This was about a few months ago. He and Lewis went out to get some wood last Saturday to sell. And you know the Krantzes?

CURTIS. You mean David Krantzes family?

GERALD. Yeah. They told my dad they would buy a cord of wood from him. Then when my dad and Lewis got back Krantz wouldn't pay for it. My dad asked him why, but Krantz said my dad was trying to steal from him and there would be no way in hell, he would buy wood from a nigger.

CURTIS. Really? After he said, he would?

GERALD. Yeah. My dad came into the house and slammed the door. All of us kids went running into the back room. But I stayed. I never did see him that way before.

CURTIS. What happened? Did he hit your mom?

GERALD. No.

CURTIS. My dad is always hitting my mom. We don't eat on time, she spills something, no money when he wants to buy beer – hits her all the time.

GERALD. No, my dad has never done anything like that. He just gets mad and walks away. But this time, he different. My mom walked over to him and tried to hug him, I guess, and then with just one arm, he threw her arms off him. Her arms just went flying. I thought he was going to hit her.

CURTIS. Did he?

GERALD. Huh-uh.

CURTIS. I bet he would've. My dad used to make sure we weren't around – now he don't even care.

GERALD. No, my dad didn't hit my mom. He grabbed her. Hugged her. Like this.

>   (**GERALD** *hugs* **CURTIS** *who is completely surprised.*)

CURTIS. Hey. Don't do that.

GERALD. Well, you asked.

CURTIS. Don't do that.

GERALD. Then, I don't know. I'm not too sure.

CURTIS. What?

GERALD. I think he started to cry.

CURTIS. Wow! Really?

GERALD. I don't know. I was hiding and could barely see them. And I could barely hear him when he talked.

CURTIS. What was he saying?

GERALD. Something about going back to Krantz and hitting him.

CURTIS. Really? Did he do it?

GERALD. No – at least I don't think so. All I remember was my mom saying, "I married and Indian man. I married an Indian man."

CURTIS. Was she crying, too?

GERALD. No. She was hugging my dad. He tried to pull her off, but he couldn't.

CURTIS. Well, my dad would've. Would've sent my mom flying across the room.

GERALD. No, my dad wouldn't do that – I think.

CURTIS. Did your dad over to Krantzes?

GERALD. No. They just stood there for a few minutes. Then she let him go and she made him something to eat.

CURTIS. Oh.

GERALD. Well, you want to go over to your house so I can get my bat?

CURTIS. Yeah. I guess.

GERALD. What's wrong?

CURTIS. I just wanted to hold on to it a couple of more days.

GERALD. Why?

CURTIS. You know, to play with it and stuff.

GERALD. But we can't. If I come over now, Gary might not be home, I won't get beat up.

CURTIS. Yeah.

GERALD. Wait. You can keep it.

CURTIS. Yeah, but I want my BB gun back.

GERALD. Yeah. You can come over and get it.

CURTIS. Maybe I can get it tomorrow.

GERALD. You sure?

CURTIS. What do want to do?

GERALD. I don't know.

CURTIS. I think – yeah, I should go home. My dad should be back by now.

GERALD. Are you going to tell?

CURTIS. What?

GERALD. Are you going to tell him about our fight?

CURTIS. No.

GERALD. What about Gary?

CURTIS. No. He'll get mad because I couldn't beat you up. He'll make fun of me and tell me I couldn't beat up a nigger.

GERALD. Yeah. I'll see you, Curtis.

CURTIS. Maybe we can play tomorrow.

GERALD. I don't know, Curtis. We should wait and see.

CURTIS. Yeah. I guess you're right. Okay. I'll see you then, tomorrow.

GERALD. Yeah. Maybe.

CURTIS. Are you going to tell Lewis?

GERALD. Yeah.

CURTIS. Why?

GERALD. Because you tried to beat me up.

CURTIS. Do you think he'll beat me up?

GERALD. No.

CURTIS. What about Gary?

GERALD. Yeah.

CURTIS. Then don't tell him, Gerald. Cause if you do, I'll get it.

GERALD. Are you crying?

CURTIS. Yeah. Because I don't want Gary to beat me up!

GERALD. Okay, Curtis, okay. I won't.

*(He slowly approaches **CURTIS** and holds him.)*

CURTIS. Promise?

GERALD. Yeah, I promise.

CURTIS. I won't listen to that dumb shit Gary again.

GERALD. Yeah, I guess you shouldn't.

CURTIS. You know what, Gerald?

GERALD. What?

CURTIS. I like you. You know what?

GERALD. No. Why?

CURTIS. Because my dad is always saying stuff about how you can't trust niggers. I trust you, Gerald.

GERALD. That's because I'm not a nigger, Curtis. I'm an Indian.

CURTIS. Yeah. Right. We're Indians. I guess we shouldn't have even been fighting, huh?

GERALD. Yeah. I guess we shouldn't be fighting.

CURTIS. Well, I'm going to go home, Gerald. See you tomorrow.

GERALD. Yeah. Bye, Curtis.

(**CURTIS** *begins to exit and comes to a stop.*)

CURTIS. And you promise you won't tell Lewis?

GERALD. Yeah. I won't. Bye.

(**CURTIS** *exits.* **GERALD** *picks up a rock and throws it. Picks up a second rock and holds on to it. He begins to shake a little and sits. Blackout.*)

End of Play

The Council

CHARACTERS

BEING ONE – Plays **MAN** and **JOEY**

BEING TWO – Plays **WHALE ONE, CONDOR, ICE TRAVELER,** and **WOMAN**

BEING THREE – Plays **SCIENTIST, SPARROW, WALRUS, MAN THREE,** and **WOLF ONE**

BEING FOUR – Plays **WHALE TWO, TIGER, SEA TURTLE, WOMAN TWO,** and **WOLF TWO**

BEING FIVE – Plays **FATHER, PANDA BEAR,** and **MAN ONE**

BEING SIX – Plays **WHALE THREE, SEA GULL, LIZARD,** and **MAN TWO**

BEING SEVEN – Plays **MICHELLE, EAGLE, WOLF, MAKO, WATER BUFFALO CALF,** and **WOMAN ONE**

AUTHOR'S NOTES

Casting

There are multiple roles. All require a great amount of physical abilities and heart.

Native characters should always be played by Native actors. The production must know whether the Native actor is an enrolled member of their tribe or of descent, and if they live their life in community as a Native person, before casting. In no instance should someone who claims to be a Native actor but who has no tribal affiliation be cast in one of these roles.

Production Elements

This play may require use of traditional items, of significant spiritual or ceremonial purposes. It may also take place in settings very specific to and known by Native peoples, and require traditional clothing or elements of regalia. All such items, settings, clothing and elements must be made appropriately. No traditional or ceremonial items should be manufactured by non-Natives. All such items, settings, clothing and elements should be thoroughly researched and accurate, and incorporate Native consultation from the specific tribes represented in the play when appropriate.

Artistic Personnel

This play should not be produced without Native voices attached to the production with a strong leadership presence in the room. In instances where a non-Native is directing, a Native dramaturg or consultant appropriate to the cultures represented in the play should be engaged. In all instances, Native cast members should be listened to and respected concerning Native representation. For the play to be truly realized, all cultural elements must be accurate. Any cultural statements, references and design elements must be accurate to the cultures they are intended to represent. There should be no compromise in ensuring that the Native peoples depicted in the play are depicted accurately, with full knowledge of the communities to which they belong.

PROLOGUE

*(There are three banners flying in the air. They represent **WHALES**. One by one the **WHALES** beach themselves on the shore. A **FATHER** and his two children, **MICHELLE** and **JOEY**, enter.)*

MICHELLE. Oh daddy, look!

JOEY. What are they, daddy?

FATHER. Whales. They must have beached themselves a few minutes ago.

MICHELLE. Are they still alive? Hey, daddy. Look at those men over there, daddy. Maybe they'll know what to do – you think so?

FATHER. Yes, maybe. Michelle and Joey, you stay here and don't touch anything. I'm going over there to ask one of those men if they know what's going on. I'll be right back.

*(The **FATHER** begins to exit, and **JOEY** follows him. The **FATHER** stops and takes **JOEY** back to **MICHELLE**.)*

I said I'll be right back.

*(He exits. Then one of the **WHALES** makes a sound.)*

MICHELLE. Do you hear that, Joey? It sounds like one of them's trying to say something.

JOEY. No they're not. You're just trying to scare me.

MICHELLE. Don't be such a geek. I am not – just listen.

WHALE ONE. A long time ago,

WHALES TOGETHER. Grandchildren,

WHALE ONE. The world was young and new. Always changing. The changes of

WHALES TOGETHER. fire, floods, earthquakes, tornadoes, hurricanes,

WHALE ONE. made the first beings join together for their own survival. It was then they decided they would have

WHALES TOGETHER. Council.

(Music as actors freeze.* Blackout.)

---

* A license to produce *The Council* does not include a performance license for any third-party or copyrighted music. Licensees should create an original composition or use music in the public domain. For further information, please see the Music and Third-Party Materials Use Note on page iii.

Scene One

*(**MAN** is onstage. He is trying to fly by flapping his arms. **SEA GULL**, **EAGLE**, **SPARROW**, and then, **CONDOR** enter. **SEA GULL** pokes **MAN** and causes a stir. They settle down to a quiet state.)*

SEA GULL. He won't, he can't, he can't fly. What a goofy being.

EAGLE. Quiet, Sea Gull.

SPARROW. There is a possibility he will go to the Council.

MAN. What's this "Council" thing, anyway? I don't want to go. I want to stay with my own nation.

CONDOR. No. We were told to bring you to the Council, Man. You have to appear before the Council. Now, climb on my back and I'll take you there.

SEA GULL. A long, a long way, a long journey to have.

MAN. From here to the Council?

SEA GULL. No, no – I mean, from Condor's back, when in the sky, to the ground is a long way to splat.

CONDOR. Don't say things like that to him! Eagle, Sparrow, help him get on my back.

EAGLE. Man, be brave. Do it now. Condor is the strongest of all of us, and she'll take you there safely.

MAN. All right. Maybe one of these days I'll make the journey myself.

*(The **BIRD BEINGS** laugh.)*

SEA GULL. Don't, don't, don fa...don't splat.

MAN. Thanks a lot.

*(The **BIRDS** begin to take off. **CONDOR** is the last to take off.)*

EAGLE. Farewell, Man.

SPARROW. Bye, oh – bye, bye, bye.

*(**CONDOR** and **MAN** are in the air.)*

MAN. This is, this is,

CONDOR. Work.

MAN. No. This is wonderful. I want – I want to fly by myself!

CONDOR. You're not made for it.

MAN. What do you mean?

CONDOR. I have feathers and the ability to fly.

MAN. If I had feathers, could I fly?

CONDOR. I don't know.

*(**MAN** examines the feathers on **CONDOR**'s back. He picks one.)*

Some of our relations have feathers and can't fly. Ow. There are some of them who are very fast runners and can't fly. Ow. What are you doing, Man?

MAN. Just borrowing some feathers.

*(**MAN** has picked several feathers, and **CONDOR** is having problems flying.)*

CONDOR. What? Ow! Why?

MAN. So I can fly by myself.

CONDOR. Man! No! You can't fly. And I can't fly if you take my feathers.

MAN. Yes, I can.

(**MAN** *takes the feathers he has plucked from* **CONDOR**, *jumps off of* **CONDOR***'s back, and tries to flap his arms.*)

I can, I can go... I'm gonna go "splat!"

(**MAN** *comes crashing to the ground. The* **COUNCIL** *gathers around him.* **CONDOR, WOLF, TIGER, PANDA BEAR, WALRUS,** *and* **LIZARD.***)*

TIGER. Members of the Council, I give you our new being, "Man."

(**WOLF** *walks over and sniffs* **MAN.***)*

WOLF. So this is how it looks up close. It's still alive.

(**MAN** *stirs, and* **WOLF** *brushes dirt on him and walks away.*)

WALRUS. Oh, bother. I was hoping this wouldn't take so long.

CONDOR. As a representative of my nation and all my relations, I thank you for the chance to bring this new being to the Council. If you don't need me for anything else, I would like to return to my home while the wind is still my relative.

TIGER. Yes – thank you, Condor. You are excused.

(**CONDOR** *exits.*)

LIZARD. What – shall we do with this – silly being?

TIGER. Lizard, my old friend, that's why we are here. All of you, Talkers from the nations and your relations, what are we to do with this new being, "Man"?

WOLF. I, Wolf, say we should get rid of him and his small herd.

TIGER. Then I take it we're in agreement not to let this being live with us?

PANDA BEAR. Excuse me, Tiger and other distinguished Talkers of the Council, but we can't do that. If a cloud passes into the empty sky, we can't prevent it from doing so. He comes from the earth just as we do.

WALRUS. Perhaps he will go away. Pass on. Remember, Panda Bear, remember Lizard's nations and all their relations had beings that passed on. Some of his relations had wings and flew in the sky, and they had no feathers. The ancient ones. They passed away – frightening beings they were. I remember hearing the story of one having little arms. He passed on as well.

WOLF. You may be right, Walrus. Man and his nations may not survive if they don't learn to feed themselves. Man's pack has been taking the remains of our hunts, but they need to learn to hunt for themselves.

TIGER. If a claw poked its skin, the skin would open. Its skin feels so thin.

WALRUS. Look! Not only is it thin skinned, but it grows plants on itself.

PANDA BEAR. Walrus, my large relation, these plants aren't growing from it. Man takes these plants to cover himself.

WOLF. Should we allow it to pass away or live amongst us?

PANDA BEAR. The Council and all the nations would have to make an exception for Man and his herd, flock, or pack. I want an agreement that we will should not hunt them until they've become larger in numbers and stronger in health.

TIGER. No. Full members of the Council hunt and are hunted, no matter what health they are. It's the circle of life...

LIZARD. They are weak of body. They could be weak of mind. If this is so, they will never learn our ways.

PANDA BEAR. We teach our cubs who are weak and don't know the ways. We can teach it the same things. Man will learn, but we have to protect this new being until it has developed its own skills and built its strength...

WALRUS. Protect it? See here, Panda Bear. No one protects our young for us. We do it.

PANDA BEAR. *(Motions to call for a vote.)* There is no other way for them to survive. Agree?

WALRUS. Oh all right, Panda Bear.

(Vote is taken and won.)

They will not be hunted.

WOLF. Will it be a Talker for itself, or should we choose a Talker for it since it is so weak?

PANDA BEAR. Wolf, it has to be able to talk for itself. It has a mouth, I think.

*(**PANDA BEAR** examines **MAN**.)*

WALRUS. Because he and his nation are so young, he should have a Talker who is already recognized and established in bloodlines to talk for him and his nation.

PANDA BEAR. Who is the closest relation to Man? Doesn't anyone want to claim relationship to this new being?

*(**WHALE** sound.)*

ICE TRAVELER. Me, me – I will.

*(**COUNCIL MEMBERS** stir.)*

PANDA BEAR. Now, this is very interesting, two relations from two different homes. Someone wants to serve as a Talker for Man. Here is Ice Traveler of the Orca nations and all their relations.

WALRUS. Ice Traveler? Oh dear. I'd rather be splatted, myself.

WOLF. Really? Who could lift you?

LIZARD. Maybe one of the ancient ones, the one with the tiny arms.

TIGER. Silence! We will meet with Ice Traveler.

> (**COUNCIL MEMBERS** *cross to the edge of the circle.* **ICE TRAVELER** *is represented by a banner.* **ICE TRAVELER** *comes to a stop and the* **COUNCIL MEMBERS** *gather near.* **MAN** *is motionless on the stage.*)

ICE TRAVELER. Members of the Council, I will see to it that Man and his nations grow strong. They will become a proud nations of the Council. We are all different, but we must live together as one, and he will be taught this. I will ask help from other Council members to teach Man and his nations to live.

> (**PANDA BEAR** *steps forward.*)

WOLF. You and Panda Bear will make sure he understands and learns the Council's ways, Ice Traveler?

ICE TRAVELER. Yes, I will. We will all teach them.

LIZARD. Silliness!

ICE TRAVELER. If I am wrong, then he will pass away like other nations of the past.

> (**MAN** *stirs, and* **COUNCIL MEMBERS** *cross to him.*)

MAN. I, me, I – I splatted. Ow! My arm is sore, too.

> (**PANDA BEAR** *is face to face with* **MAN**.)

What? I, I – I mean, who are you?

PANDA BEAR. Panda Bear, Talker of the Panda Bear nation and all their relations.

MAN. The Council. I made it? I didn't think I would get here.

PANDA BEAR. Yes. Would you like to wrestle? Best two out of three?

MAN. No, no – thank you, but nah. Uh – am I and my people to be included in the Council? We can use more help. Wolf and her nations have been helpful in providing food, but we don't get enough to eat. We are the fourth ones to eat after Wolf and the other nations.

PANDA BEAR. Man, you'll be heard and fed. Things will change for you and your people. Your markings will soon join ours in the Council circle.

> (**MAN** *walks around the circle. He is about to place his handprint.*)

Wait, – you'll have to wait.

MAN. Uh – I thank you, all of you. I'm, uh – I'm going to get something to sit on.

> (**MAN** *exits offstage. The* **COUNCIL MEMBERS** *re-form into* **COUNCIL** *stances in a circle.*)

TIGER. Members of the Council, when Man has grown, we will allow him to place his markings at the edge of the Council circle with ours. Then he will become the Talker of his nation and join the circle of life.

> (**MAN** *enters with a small hide. This causes a large uproar among the* **COUNCIL MEMBERS** *until* **TIGER** *restores order.*)

WOLF. Look!

TIGER. What is that?

PANDA BEAR. Answer, Man.

MAN. I needed something to sit on. The idea came to me, so I'm going to use this mangy old hide.

TIGER. Where did you get – get this "hide"?

MAN. From over there. There were a lot of them.

WALRUS. That hide is from the resting place of the Council members we honor.

COUNCIL MEMBERS. Man! Silliness! Silly Thing! Strange Being! Greedy pup!

(Blackout.)

Scene Two

(**TIGER** *is hiding in some bushes.* **MAN** *and* **PANDA BEAR** *enter. When they do,* **TIGER** *stalks them.*)

PANDA BEAR. You are fortunate that no being is allowed to be attacked or hunted at a Council. Be sure to think before you take.

(**TIGER** *charges out and knocks* **MAN** *down.*)

TIGER. What – what a strange cub. So skinny.

PANDA BEAR. Now, first we are going to have Tiger teach you how to hunt. That will be your first path to learning the ways of this world. Kill only to hunt and to protect.

MAN. Hunt? Oh, you mean to get food?

TIGER. You have to eat, don't you? Where is your partner?

MAN. Don't have one. Why should I have one?

TIGER. No wonder you're starving.

PANDA BEAR. First you must know what fills your stomach.

MAN. You mean, what is it we eat?

TIGER. Yes.

MAN. Do you have any grubs and twigs in this land?

TIGER. Grubs and twigs? You'll feed a whole family and a nation on twigs and grubs?

MAN. Everything else is too fast or too big for us to hunt.

TIGER. Then I will show you how to hunt those who are too fast and too big for you to catch.

MAN. All right. "Hear me, O too big and too fast" …

TIGER. Silence! Silence! Now, there is a water buffalo calf over there.

MAN. Really? Where?

TIGER. Smell it.

MAN. I can't smell it. Are you sure…

TIGER. Will you be silent! Shhh – it's coming this way.

MAN. What are you going to do when it gets here?

TIGER. I will surprise it and jump on it. I'll go for its neck and then bring it down – humph! And what will you do, Man?

MAN. Oh – run like a four-legged ostrich in the other direction.

TIGER. No, no. You will come from the other side. Now watch closely. Soon it will come out of the weeds, and you'll have something for your family to eat.

> *(She exits into the bushes. **MAN** doesn't. **TIGER** chases **MAN** to **PANDA BEAR**, who is hiding in the bushes. She returns to her hiding place.)*

MAN. Panda Bear, I don't know if I can do it.

PANDA BEAR. Shhh – trust her, Man. She is a great hunter for her nation.

MAN. Yes, but she has things. She has claws, teeth, and a lot of other things I don't have.

PANDA BEAR. You have claws.

> *(**PANDA BEAR** examines **MAN**'s hands.)*

Or the beginnings of claws. You have teeth.

MAN. But I can't do what she does. I need something else.

> *(He begins to look around the bushes. He finds a stick and a rock, and then a vine.)*

PANDA BEAR. Now what are you doing, Man? Man?

(**MAN** *places the rock on the stick and uses the vine to wrap the rock to the stick.*)

MAN. Making a claw.

(*From another part of the stage,* **WATER BUFFALO CALF** *enters.* **TIGER** *takes a sniff.*)

WATER BUFFALO CALF. Ma? Ma? Ma? Ma? Ma?

(**TIGER** *stalks* **WATER BUFFALO CALF**, *but before she can attack,* **MAN** *charges and strikes* **TIGER** *with the claw and then gives a loud charging cry and chases* **WATER BUFFALO CALF** *offstage.* **PANDA BEAR** *and* **TIGER** *freeze, watching him, and then look at each other.*)

TIGER. He can't be taught anything.

PANDA BEAR. He was only trying to help you.

TIGER. Now what do I feed my family?

PANDA BEAR. He didn't mean to ruin your hunt. I'm sure he'll take responsibility for what he's done.

TIGER. I should feed him to my family.

PANDA BEAR. Remember our agreement. Man is not to be hunted.

TIGER. Then you teach him how to hunt.

(*She exits.* **MAN** *enters with a melon.*)

MAN. Look – look what I knocked out of a tree with my claw.

(*Proudly displays his club.*)

Now I have to work on making myself some teeth. Where's Tiger?

PANDA BEAR. She's not – not too pleased at this moment.

MAN. It wasn't my fault. She got in my way.

PANDA BEAR. Oh, Man. You have a lot to learn about the hunt. I still think you should learn to, to – to wrestle.

> *(He playfully charges* **MAN**. **MAN** *doesn't know what to do, but he raises the club in defense.* **PANDA BEAR** *senses the pose and withdraws.* **MAN** *drops the melon and the club and runs to* **PANDA BEAR**. *They embrace.* **PANDA BEAR** *laughs. Blackout.)*

Scene Three

(ICE TRAVELER and SEA TURTLE are onstage. ICE TRAVELER is in the water and SEA TURTLE is on the beach.)

SEA TURTLE. Lizard didn't agree with my helping you, Ice Traveler, but you, I like you. Just call me.

ICE TRAVELER. Like this?

(Whale sound.)

SEA TURTLE. Beautiful.

ICE TRAVELER. Thank you, Sea Turtle. Man must learn about other nations and where they live.

(MAN enters, carrying a lance.)

MAN. Hello, Ice Traveler, and – and, whatever you, uh – hi.

ICE TRAVELER. Hello. This is my friend, Sea Turtle. Today we have another kind of world to show you, one called "ocean," which we call home.

SEA TURTLE. I don't wish to sound bothersome, but what is that thing you are carrying?

MAN. It's something new I've made. I have watched other beings hunt with their large teeth. My teeth are small. This will be my tooth – my people call it a "spear" – and now I can take bigger bites.

SEA TURTLE. You still eat? You can bite things?

MAN. But they are little bites.

SEA TURTLE. Then eat only little things.

MAN. I can't survive eating only little things.

SEA TURTLE. Why not? Many of Ice Traveler's relations do.

MAN. Not me.

SEA TURTLE. Why?

MAN. Uh, uh – because!

SEA TURTLE. Oh. I can see a glimmer of understanding there.

ICE TRAVELER. A second way of the Council says, if you go into land marked by another nation, you respect that home and don't leave your markings there.

MAN. This'll be easy. It's only water.

SEA TURTLE. Hmmm, there could be a problem here. The ocean is home to many nations, Man.

ICE TRAVELER. You'll understand it better when you see what we mean, Man. Now, let's start while we still have the sun.

(**MAN** *tries to get into the water.*)

SEA TURTLE. Man, you may ride beside me or on my back. Whatever is easier for you.

MAN. Thank you, Sea Turtle.

(**MAN** *jumps on* **SEA TURTLE***'s back. They go underwater and reappear.*)

Are we going far?

ICE TRAVELER. Oh yes.

MAN. This water feels funny.

ICE TRAVELER. It is very different from the water you find on land. I'm going ahead of you and Man, Sea Turtle. I want to make sure the path is clear.

(*Whale sound.* **ICE TRAVELER** *exits.*)

SEA TURTLE. Don't go too far, Ice Traveler.

(**WALRUS** *enters. He is fishing.*)

WALRUS. Hello, Sea Turtle.

SEA TURTLE. Hello, Walrus.

WALRUS. Is that your new offspring? Seems to have lost his shell.

SEA TURTLE. We're busy Walrus. Man? How do you move in the water?

MAN. I can move fine.

SEA TURTLE. Wonderful, because I'm getting a little weary of carrying you.

> (**SEA TURTLE** *dumps* **MAN** *into the water.* **MAN** *panics.*)

MAN. Help! I'll be – I'll be swallowed. Help me!

SEA TURTLE. Don't be ridiculous. A little water never hurt anyone...

WALRUS. Odd being.

MAN. Help!

> (*Swims to* **WALRUS**, *who splashes him with water.*)

WALRUS. A bit awkward.

SEA TURTLE. Now, now – remain calm. You'll be all right. Just move your fins, uh whatever those things are called.

MAN. Hands.

SEA TURTLE. Yes, your fins and hands.

> (**WALRUS** *goes underwater and gets a fish.*)

WALRUS. Delightful hunting today, don't you think?

> (*Plays with fish.*)

MAN. Hey. That's my fish.

SEA TURTLE. We share, Man. There is enough for everyone.

(**SEA TURTLE** *goes under and gets a fish for* **MAN**.)

Here.

MAN. But I want that one.

WALRUS. This one? But why?

SEA TURTLE. Yes, why?

MAN. Because, uh – because it's mine!

WALRUS. Oh, very well – here.

(**WALRUS** *throws a fish at* **MAN**. *It hits him.*)

MAN. Ow! Hey, you big – you big slug.

(**WALRUS** *puts his fin on top of* **MAN**'s *head and holds him underwater.*)

WALRUS. Rude little being.

(**WALRUS** *lets* **MAN** *up.*)

Reminds me of the time when I was...

(**WALRUS** *releases* **MAN** *and sees* **MAKO**'s *fin.*)

Oh – oh. An unwanted visitor. Shark! Swim everyone. Swim away.

(**WALRUS** *exits.* **MAKO** *swims around upstage of* **SEA TURTLE** *and* **MAN**.)

MAN. He doesn't frighten me. I have my tooth, you know. No one is going to take my lunch.

SEA TURTLE. Oh no! Mako, listen to me! You must not attack us, because – uh, because...

MAN. Just because.

SEA TURTLE. No, because we're teaching the new being.

MAKO. Is it tasty? Crunchy, munchy new being. Tasty new being, is it?

MAN. I'm not afraid of him.

> (**MAN** *takes his spear and lunges it forward into* **MAKO**'s *mouth.* **MAKO** *is hurt, then spits out the spear.*)

MAKO. It tastes stringy. New being, new being, is that your name? We want to remember you. That way, the next time we meets one of you, we'll know how tasty you all are when we eats you.

MAN. Help!

SEA TURTLE. I thought you said you weren't afraid.

MAN. That was before he took my tooth.

SEA TURTLE & MAN. Help! Ice Traveler! Help!

MAKO. We think we'll have a few fins, tasty, munchy finnies, then the new being. All very tasty and very munchy crunchy.

> (**MAKO** *is ready to make his attack, but* **ICE TRAVELER** *arrives and bumps him. He doesn't see* **ICE TRAVELER**.)

Eeee! What is the cause of our hurt? What takes us away from our crunchy munchies?

ICE TRAVELER. These beings are protected by the "Council."

MAKO. Council? Yes – we remembers Council. Who cares for the Council? No one tells us whens to eats. We eats whatever is crunchies and munchiest, babe!

ICE TRAVELER. If you don't leave them alone, I will bump you and bite you.

MAKO. We goes, we goes, nice-eties lady.

(Begins to exit but stops near **MAN**.*)*

MAKO. Stay healthies – we don't likes excess fats.

*(***MAKO*** exits.)*

SEA TURTLE. If you are to fear anything in the world of water, he and all his nations and their relations are the ones to fear, Man. Brutes is what they are.

MAN. The nations should get together and kick them out of the Council.

ICE TRAVELER. No. This is Mako's home, and he belongs here. He has a purpose to the earth as everyone else does. There are good beings like us and then there are those like Mako. They are old members of the Council, but as time went on they grew in numbers, Mako's brain never changed.

SEA TURTLE. I'm surprised he still remembers the word, "Council."

MAN. Ice Traveler? There are a lot of water beings I haven't met. How do I know which ones to fear and which ones not to?

ICE TRAVELER. Try not to fear other beings, Man. You will know the ones to stay away from and the ones to go to when you're in trouble and need help. Just be watchful.

SEA TURTLE. Here – get on my back. Man – you're heavy. You should eat little things.

(Blackout.)

Scene Four

> (**WOMAN** *is standing near a small stream. She has a spear and is fishing. There are some tall reeds nearby. When she is gong to strike,* **MAN** *enters. He is wearing a headdress made of flowers and weeds.* **WOMAN** *hides behind the reeds and watches.)*

MAN. I am Man, small water beings. I have come to get you to eat you. Now, do not make me use my tooth. Come out of your homes now!

> (**WOMAN** *crosses to* **MAN** *and thumps him in the rear with her spear.)*

Ow! Who – who are you?

WOMAN. A being trying to get some food. You scared my food away.

MAN. Not me. I'm getting food for myself.

> (**WOMAN** *pointing at the headdress.)*

WOMAN. What's that?

MAN. This? This is to let everyone know that I'm the leader of the nation of Man.

WOMAN. That's very funny. Now, who – what are you?

MAN. Let me introduce myself. Ahem, I am Man. I can talk with all the beings of the Council. Do not fear me, because – I don't fear you. Because I can talk to all the beings of the Council and be heard, I am a leader – a "Talker."

WOMAN. Then go and "talk" somewhere else. I need to eat.

MAN. I – I can help you. I can get food to feed you.

WOMAN. So can I. Man – are you always this noisy when you hunt?

(He begins to jump into the stream.)

MAN. No. Just watch. Watch how great – good, I am – was...

WOMAN. You'll scare them away.

MAN. Come here, fish beings!

WOMAN. Here. I'll show you how to do it.

(She leads him out of the stream with her spear, then spears a fish.)

MAN. Uh, that one must have heard me.

(They stand looking at the fish.)

Looks like it's some good food.

WOMAN. Would you like to share my food? I don't think I can eat all this by myself.

MAN. Sure.

(He removes the fish from the spear and takes a bite out of it.)

WOMAN. What are you doing?

MAN. Eating.

WOMAN. The head? Not even prepared! Yuck!

MAN. How else do you eat a water being?

WOMAN. You can eat it raw, but you have to prepare it first. You could season it with some herbs, broast it, roast it, fry it, dry it...

MAN. All right. Prepare it! Puh-lease?

WOMAN. Just this once, but you have to clean up after we're done.

(They play around and it leads to a kiss. They break off awkwardly.)

MAN. Yes, uh – my name is Man. What's yours?

WOMAN. Woman.

MAN. You're nice. Gentle, too.

WOMAN. You're strange – and gentle, I guess.

(She begins to exit. He follows.)

MAN. We can get a lot of things done together, can't we?

WOMAN. After watching you, I don't know.

*(**MAN** leaves her and jumps back into the stream.)*

MAN. Hear me, O fish beings. One of you is our meal for today. You should all feel good about that. Next time when I call, I want you all to be ready to...

WOMAN. Are you hungry, or do you want to talk?

MAN. I'm hungry, but I want more fish. Not for me, but for us.

WOMAN. We already have fish for lunch and some other food we can share. Man? If you get more fish... Stupid Man!

(He doesn't pay attention to her as she exits.)

MAN. Come here, O fish beings.

*(**MAN** tries to get one and misses.)*

If there was only a way of stopping you guys from getting away. Ha!

*(**MAN** takes a stone sitting near the bank and rolls it into the stream. Then finds another stone and does the same.)*

MAN. Now, you'll have to come to me, O fish beings.

> (*Picks fish out of the water and tosses it onto the bank.* **WOLF** *enters and watches him. She slowly sneaks near him.* **MAN** *finally discovers her.*)

WOLF. Hello, Man. That is a lot of fish you have. I'm hungry. You will not mind if I...

MAN. No, Wolf.

WOLF. But Man, we've always shared our food with you.

MAN. After you ate first and took all the good parts.

WOLF. Then I'll wait, like you did.

MAN. No. Get away from me.

> (**WOLF** *picks up a fish.*)

Put that down! You can't have any.

> (**MAN** *picks up a rock and throws it.*)

WOLF. Ow! Man!

> (**WOLF** *drops the fish.* **MAN** *gets more rocks to throw.*)

MAN. Go on.

WOLF. You're supposed to share with – ow – others.

MAN. Leave!

WOLF. Stop it!

> (**WOLF** *exits.* **MAN** *slowly gets out of the stream, gathers his fish, and cautiously looks around. He leaves the stream blocked and exits. Blackout.*)

Scene Five

(**MAN** *is kneeling. In front of him is a small pile of twigs. He has two rocks and is rubbing the rocks together.* **WOMAN** *enters. She is listening to the sounds around her. She crosses to him.*)

WOMAN. Do you think they will come, Man?

MAN. I don't see why not. Don't be afraid. They are my friends. Why, I'm nearly one of them. When they see this new gift I have for them, they'll be so surprised they'll want to make me a Head Talker.

(**WOLF** *enters and howls. The* **PANDA BEAR** *and* **LIZARD** *enter.* **TIGER** *enters and brushes past* **WOMAN**.)

TIGER. Man, why have you called us to the dens of your nation?

LIZARD. Yes. What is wrong? Cannot drink from the stream because it moves too fast for you?

MAN. Wait. You'll see. I have something I want to share with you animals.

PANDA BEAR. We – "animals"? What does "animals" mean?

MAN. I mean, we, "my" nation, are "human beings," and you are just beings – "animals."

PANDA BEAR. Excuse me, but then if we are just beings and you are a being; you're an animal too.

MAN. Okay. I'm a "human animal." Now I have something I want to share with the nations of the Council. It's something I've found. We're using it in our den areas and it's great.

TIGER. We have something to say to you, Man. You must obey the ways…

MAN. Yes, yes, yes. Let me show you this first.

> (**TIGER** *is angered.*)

PANDA BEAR. Man, please listen to Tiger. We've all come a long way to...

MAN. I will, I will. Just wait up.

> (**TIGER** *rushes* **MAN** *and knocks him over. This catches everyone off guard.*)

TIGER. MAN! Man, you and your nation must obey the Council's ways.

MAN. All right, Tiger, all right – good kitty – but you got to see this first.

> (*He goes back to his rocks and the small pile of twigs.* **TIGER** *signals* **WOLF**, *and they both start to stalk* **MAN**. *Just when they are ready to attack,* **WOMAN** *helps* **MAN** *by striking the rocks together and making a spark for the fire.* **MAN** *picks up one of the lit pieces of wood.*)

Behold. I give the nations, uh – "something that's red and hot."

> (**MAN** *drives off* **WOLF** *and* **TIGER**.)

Don't be afraid of it. It won't bite. Ha!

PANDA BEAR. Excuse me, Man, but we call this "fire."

MAN. "Fire"? You know about this stuff already?

WOLF. We have known about it for many seasons.

> (**MAN** *walks around holding the flaming piece of wood. He chases off* **TIGER**.)

MAN. Do you want some fire? What about you?

LIZARD. Excuse me, but get rid of the fire, Man. REMOVE IT NOW!

MAN. This is a gift. It's a gift from my nation to the nations of the Council.

> (**WOMAN** *crosses to* **MAN** *and tries to stop him from terrorizing everybody.*)

WOMAN. Maybe you're holding it to close to them?

MAN. I know what I'm doing with it. There's nothing to be afraid of.

> (**WOLF** *grabs a hold of* **LIZARD**'s *tail.*)

WOLF. He will hurt all of us. Run! Run!

> (**WOLF** *drags* **LIZARD** *offstage.* **MAN** *follows them.*)

MAN. No! Stay! It's safe. Panda Bear, Panda Bear – make them stay. It won't hurt them.

> (*Crosses to* **PANDA BEAR** *and prevents him from escaping.*)

PANDA BEAR. Put it down, Man. Put the fire down.

MAN. All right.

> (*He mindlessly tosses the burning piece of wood. Fire starts in the area and grows. All three turn to look. [The fire can be represented by red banners.]*)

Oh, oh.

PANDA BEAR. What?

MAN. Run!

> (*Three large banners representing fire appear onstage and circle the stage area.* **WOLF** *enters*

and dances with the banners. One banner disappears, and **WOLF** *now takes the time to catch her breath.)*

WOLF. Hurry! Stay with your clan. You will survive this if you stay with your clan.

*(**WOLF** fights the banners and **TIGER** enters challenging the flames.)*

TIGER. Those of you who can't run, go to the streams and rivers. Hurry! It's getting closer.

*(She fights off the flames and gets near **WOLF**.)*

I want to meet with all the Talkers as soon as we have outdistanced the fire.

*(**TIGER** is nearly ready to run when **SPARROW** flies in and catches her attention.)*

SPARROW. Tiger, Tiger! I see – I see the fire.

TIGER. How large is it?

SPARROW. It is large, yes – oh, oh, very large.

TIGER. Will we be able to escape it?

SPARROW. Yes, Man helps. Man and his nation helps – helps me, helps us. We can escape. They are on the other side of the fire.

TIGER. His families and relatives are safe.

SPARROW. They're tossing dirt and water on the fire – on the fire, oh my.

TIGER. What?

SPARROW. Yes. They're throwing, kicking, splashing dirt and water on the fire – oh yes, yes. We can escape, escape.

(SPARROW flies off, and WOLF joins TIGER.)

WOLF. Now is the time. We have to do something about Man. This is more of his irresponsibility.

TIGER. Not here. When we meet we'll do something about Man. Now go. Go!

(They fight off the flames. The flames change direction, and MAN and WOMAN enter.)

MAN. More water! Use the drinking water! Wet the cloth and beat the fire with it.

WOMAN. Man, we can try to change the direction of the fire.

MAN. To the river! Try to lead the fire to the river.

WOMAN. Look at what we've done. All the homes are being destroyed.

MAN. I didn't mean this to happen.

(MAN and WOMAN exit. There is one big flash of the red banner. The sounds of the fire fade. PANDA BEAR, LIZARD, WOLF, and WALRUS enter. They are tired and hurt. They try to take care of one another. TIGER enters and examines each COUNCIL MEMBER.)

TIGER. We have time now. I want you, the Talkers, to take back what is decided here and share it with your relations. Man and his nations have broken the ways. They are now large and strong and grow fat. They are now a full nation. They should be hunted.

PANDA BEAR. This is wrong, Tiger. They aren't strong enough. It's not too late to teach them the ways. We are still responsible for them.

WOLF. Responsible? Man is not responsible.

TIGER. We never know what he will do next. That is the danger.

WALRUS. That's correct. If you've noticed, Man and his nation are now quite large. They have knives, spears, and other things – I don't know what they call them, but they are dangerous to all of us.

LIZARD. They disregard the Council's ways as if the ways don't include them.

TIGER. Something has to be done. My nation and I will not wait for the next danger.

PANDA BEAR. Don't do this, Tiger. Please. We aren't like Mako and his relations. We give the ways time to work. Things will change. They have worked before. I ask all of you to please wait and be patient. Let time show us how things will work out.

TIGER. I say we don't have time. We have to act now.

WALRUS. I agree with Tiger, Panda Bear. We must act now or it'll be too late, and they'll destroy all of us.

PANDA BEAR. I don't believe hunting Man and his nation will solve the problems we face.

TIGER. We don't have time. If we wait, we will pass away, one nation after another.

WALRUS. Then is it settled? Do we agree to allow Man and his nations to be hunted like all the members of the Council?

LIZARD. Yes.

WOLF. Before it becomes too late for all of us.

> *(They call for a vote.* **PANDA BEAR** *withdraws from the vote.)*

TIGER. Let's begin now.

> *(They vote, then* **TIGER** *begins to exit.)*

PANDA BEAR. Stop, Tiger. I can't allow you to do this.

TIGER. Move out of my path, Panda Bear. It is Man I want.

PANDA BEAR. Then I cannot move. It's wrong, what you are going to do.

TIGER. I hunt to protect. For the survival of my nation.

> (**TIGER** *stalks and circles* **PANDA BEAR.** *All the* **COUNCIL MEMBERS** *become excited as the possible fight builds.*)

WALRUS. No. Not at a Council meeting. Stop, both of you!

LIZARD. Young one, don't hinder her. She says it is for protection. This is reason enough.

> (**TIGER** *and* **PANDA BEAR** *fight, exchanging blows.* **WOLF** *helps* **TIGER** *by distracting* **PANDA BEAR.** **TIGER** *charges* **PANDA BEAR** *and knocks him down to the ground. She is ready to strike his neck but stops.*)

TIGER. Hear me! Let your nations know that Man is to be hunted. If anyone in your nations is hurt or killed by Man and his nation, Man will answer to me!

> (*Blackout.*)

Scene Six

(**WOMAN** *is working in a small garden patch.* **MAN** *sneaks up behind her to surprise her. He does and she reacts by sweeping him off his feet.*)

WOMAN. Man? Oh, Man. I have something for you to do. Are you all right?

MAN. Don't worry about me. I'm like a rock.

(*Falls over after she has sat him up.*)

WOMAN. Good. I want you to help me pull out the weeds so the vegetables can grow. Do it like this.

(*Demonstrates how to pull weeds.*)

Oh – you're going to find these little bugs.

MAN. "Little beings."

WOMAN. Yes. I want you to remove them from the plants. When you finish, we'll eat.

MAN. Will I have to wash my hands before we eat – again?

WOMAN. Yes.

(*He begins to lick his hands.*)

Not like that.

MAN. All right.

(**WOMAN** *begins to exit, but stops. She watches* **MAN**.)

Weeds, weeds – which are the plants and which are the weeds?

(**WOLF ONE** *appears and begins to growl.*)

WOMAN. Listen. What is that, Man?

> (**WOLF TWO** *appears and growls.*)

MAN. Hello.

> (*Gets to his feet and walks to the* **WOLVES**.)

What's wrong? Don't you two know who I am?

> (**WOMAN** *pulls* **MAN** *back behind her.*)

WOMAN. Yes, I believe they don't know who you are.

> (**WOLF THREE** *enters. The* **WOLVES** *circle and growl at* **MAN** *and* **WOMAN**.)

MAN. Wait a minute. You beings are scouting.

WOMAN. Scouting for what?

MAN. Hunting. Wait. Your nations can't hunt us.

> (**MAN TWO** *enters, carrying a rock and a spear. He attacks the* **WOLVES** *with his spear.*)

MAN TWO. Get out of here, you bad animals! Get away from here! Go!

> (**MAN TWO** *chases them off.*)

MAN. What you doing? Come back here.

WOMAN. Were they hunting us? I thought we were not to be hunted.

MAN. Yes. I was told by the Council we would have a chance to grow.

> (**SEA GULL** *enters.*)

SEA GULL. Oh Man, oh Man, oh Man is in for it now.

WOMAN. What's it saying, Man?

SEA GULL. I hate, I wouldn't – I wouldn't want to be in your nest.

MAN. Sea Gull, what are you talking about?

SEA GULL. Good shape, good shape. Need to stay in good shape for the hunt. I don't want to be near you. Might, would, could, mistake me for you. Get away, get away, get lost, Man.

>   (**MAN TWO** *enters and stalks* **SEA GULL**.*)*

WOMAN. What about the wolves? Ask him if that's what the wolves were doing?

>   (**MAN TWO** *smacks* **SEA GULL**'s *bottom with his spear, sending* **SEA GULL** *into* **MAN** *and* **WOMAN**. **SEA GULL** *bounces off* **MAN** *and* **WOMAN** *and falls back into a waiting kick by* **MAN TWO**.*)*

MAN TWO. Get! Get away, you disgusting bird!

>   (**MAN TWO** *chases* **SEA GULL**.*)*

SEA GULL. Bad, bad, evil Man.

MAN. Sea Gull, wait! You shouldn't have done that. He wasn't bothering anyone.

MAN TWO. Oh – I save both of your lives and that's how you say thanks.

MAN. What's going on?

MAN TWO. We're being attacked! Animals have crashed into the village, biting, scratching, and slashing at everything in sight. It's terrible. At least, that's what I've heard. Move.

MAN. Who told you to do that?

>   (**MAN THREE** *enters, carrying some spears.)*

MAN THREE. Get more rocks. Tell the people to get all their knives, spears, and bows ready. We'll show these animals.

(**MAN THREE** *exits and* **MAN ONE** *enters.*)

MAN. Wait! What's going on?

MAN THREE. What are you two doing standing around? Get busy. We have to defend our villages.

MAN. From what? Ourselves?

MAN THREE. The animals.

(**WOMAN TWO** *enters being playfully chased by* **TIGER**.)

WOMAN ONE. Help me! Help me!

MAN THREE. Attack the tiger! Drive it back!

(**MAN THREE** *and* **MAN ONE** *drive* **TIGER** *offstage.* **MAN** *gets in between them.*)

MAN. That's a Talker of the Council. Don't hurt her.

WOMAN ONE. Thank you, thank you.

(*She crosses to* **MAN THREE**, *but he pushes her off to* **WOMAN**.)

MAN THREE. What are you doing? You're sympathizing with the animals! After this poor woman was attacked?

MAN. Yes – I mean, no. Listen. This is getting too crazy. We aren't being attacked. We're being hunted, that's all.

MAN THREE. But you told us we weren't to be hunted.

(**MAN TWO** *and* **WOMAN THREE** *enter.*)

MAN. I know, I know. Uh – maybe we've been doing things wrong. We have to follow the Council's ways. Have we? If we haven't, we're gong to have to stop what we're doing today and go back to the old ways.

MAN TWO. What? We can't go back to the old times, because we're too large in numbers. We've made families live in one dent until it can't hold anymore. We're now growing so large, our towns have become dirty and overcrowded.

MAN. If we're going to build more, we have to be certain the trees we take won't destroy someone's home. We have to honor the markings of other nations. It's one of the Council's ways.

WOMAN TWO. I have to let my children freeze in the snow and rain so some bird or squirrel or raccoon is safe? No! I have to take trees to build onto the home I have.

MAN. What – what about food? We all have enough to make it through this season. So if anyone hunts, we can share...

WOMAN TWO. Maybe you have enough to eat, but I don't.

MAN THREE. We are just as large as they are in numbers. They should change their ways and listen to us. We could add some new ways so we could live together.

MAN. If it weren't for them, we wouldn't have survived or grown to what we are today.

MAN THREE. But we have survived, and we should have a say in what we do. We are people, human beings. We are the new beings who will rule this world. We have ways – "laws."

MAN. Laws? What are those?

MAN THREE. Laws are the rules of how the nations of Man will live and how the nations of the Council will live under Man.

MAN. We can't change the ways overnight. The ways have been here for ages. Longer then any of us have.

MAN THREE. The laws will give us harmony with the animals. The first law is, Man can kill for food, to protect, to secure his property, and when he feels the urge. Second, all animals are beneath Man and should obey and serve Man. Third, Man has the right to use the trees, waters, air, and ground to enrich life for himself and his family. And finally, Man has the right to enter any territory or home that belongs to an animal and makes it his property.

*(Some of the **PEOPLE** respond with cheers.)*

WOMAN THREE. No, no. These laws don't sound fair to me. What about the children and women?

MAN THREE. They will be included in the laws as well, under Man.

WOMAN ONE. I can't live like that. No one should live like that.

MAN THREE. You will. You all will. If there are those of you who believe in what I say, go back to your homes and get your knives and spears.

MAN TWO. Let's do it.

WOMAN. Stop. It isn't right. We are a nation of the Council. We have to keep the Council's ways.

WOMAN ONE. Yes. We've come so far from where we used to be...

MAN THREE. Quiet! We will not be attacked by these animals!

MAN. Listen to me. Wait. Let me – let me try to call for a Council, and all of you can come with me. We'll go to the Council and ask them not to hunt us, or just give us some more time. And maybe have the laws included with the ways.

*(**MAN THREE** stalks **WOMAN**.)*

WOMAN. Yes. Man is trying to do the best for all of us. We should...

(**MAN THREE** *grabs her.*)

WOMAN. Let go of me!

MAN. This is going too far.

(**MAN THREE** *signals* **MAN ONE** *and* **MAN TWO** *to hold* **MAN** *back by spear point.*)

MAN THREE. Stay back, Man. You stay away from the Council. If you go there, you'll never see Woman again. Take her and put her behind the wall with us. You others, take Man and put him outside of the wall. Hurry! Do as I say!

MAN. But the Council will help us. I have to go.

WOMAN. Run, Man! Don't worry about me.

MAN THREE. Stop. Because if you do, you'll pay for it. Everyone at the Council will pay for their betrayal of us.

(**MAN** *is held at bay by* **MAN TWO** *and* **MAN ONE**. *He knocks their spears away and exits.*)

You fools. Don't stand there. Follow him and find out where he goes. We'll find those beasts and teach them to obey.

(**MAN ONE** *runs after* **MAN**. *Blackout.*)

Scene Seven

(**LIZARD** *is flying on the back of* **CONDOR**. **CONDOR** *makes a turn in the sky, and* **LIZARD** *doesn't follow. He floats for a moment and then falls.*)

LIZARD. Oh, oh... Ow!

(**TIGER, PANDA BEAR,** *and* **WALRUS** *enter.*)

TIGER. Lizard? Are you all right?

LIZARD. Silliness.

TIGER. Where are Man and Ice Traveler?

LIZARD. Just plain silliness.

PANDA BEAR. At least you came in a thud and not a splat.

TIGER. Man? Ice Traveler? This is useless. Where are those two?

(**WOLF** *enters.*)

WOLF. A pack of men surrounds the Council.

WALRUS. How dare they?

(**COUNCIL MEMBERS** *are upset.* **MAN** *enters, riding on the back of* **ICE TRAVELER**. **MAN** *calls out to the* **COUNCIL MEMBERS**.)

MAN. Members of the Council, hear me.

ICE TRAVELER. We have very little time. Everyone listen to him.

MAN. We must have new ways.

TIGER. What? What are they saying?

PANDA BEAR. Slow down, Man. Catch your breath. We can't understand you.

*(**MAN** has landed and crosses to the center.)*

MAN. My people – my people will hurt us if we don't obey their laws.

LIZARD. Now it's "we." When did you decide to become one of us?

MAN. They want their laws included in the ways. We have to do it, if we all want to live in peace.

WOLF. Do you really talk for your nation? Is it going to be safe here?

*(Reaction from the **COUNCIL MEMBERS**.)*

MAN. All you have to do is include some of their laws in the ways of the Council. It will be a peace offering to my nation.

LIZARD. What? Wait. What are laws, Man?

MAN. One law says we aren't going to be your equals.

TIGER. I like that. This could be interesting. What else?

MAN. We aren't going to be below you.

PANDA BEAR. Then what you going to be?

MAN. Above you.

*(**COUNCIL MEMBERS** are angered.)*

They believe they are the new beings, beings of Man. They will one-day rule over you and your nations.

TIGER. We can't accept this.

ICE TRAVELER. But it could bring peace to all of us. There is a danger rising, and we must stop it.

PANDA BEAR. This is not natural. One being more important than another? The ways have always kept the nations together as one.

MAN. Wait, wait – that's just one of their laws. Listen, if you adapt the laws into the Council's ways, we'll have peace and the Council will survive.

TIGER. Don't worry about the Council, Man. We already have peace and harmony.

> (*Signals for the* **COUNCIL** *meeting to begin, and the* **MEMBERS** *assume their positions in the circle.*)

Now, everyone knows that no one is to be hunted going to or leaving a Council, but there are some men of your nations who are doing this.

MAN. I'll tell them to go home. Just please allow them to have some of their laws.

LIZARD. Man. The Council's ways is "Kill only for food or to protect," not "Kill because you can't get have what you want."

WOLF. Or "Kill because someone doesn't agree with you."

LIZARD. If we accept your laws, will this make your people stop hunting us?

MAN. I don't know if they will.

WALRUS. Then I say no to your laws. Members of the Council, do you agree?

> (**COUNCIL MEMBERS** *begin to vote.*)

MAN. Help me, Ice Traveler.

ICE TRAVELER. Listen to me.

> (*Vote is completed.*)

TIGER. It has been decided, Ice Traveler.

> (**WALRUS** *exits.*)

ICE TRAVELER. All of Man's laws can't be bad. They are something we should consider. These are new times for all of us. There have been so many changes, and the world is unbalanced. If we could help Man, these laws could be a way to restore the harmony we've had.

TIGER. The Council has done what it could to help Man and his nation. It is enough.

> *(There is a flash of a red banner and muffled sounds.)*

Be still.

WOLF. What's wrong?

> *(**PANDA BEAR** sniffs the air.)*

PANDA BEAR. F-f-fire!

WOLF. They are breaking the circle of life.

> *(The **COUNCIL MEMBERS** scatter except **TIGER, ICE TRAVELER,** and **MAN**.)*

MAN THREE. *(From offstage.)* Get those beasts. Hurry! Don't let any of them escape. Kill them if you have too. We will end the Council.

MAN. No! You can't do this! Not here.

> *(**TIGER** stalks.)*

TIGER. You and your nations have gone too far.

ICE TRAVELER. Run, Tiger. Don't hurt him. It's not his fault.

MAN. Please, Tiger. Don't hurt me.

TIGER. How can a pitiful being like you force me to change into something I don't want to be.

> *(**TIGER** lunges at **MAN** and misses.)*

I will never be the same because of you, but this time, you'll answer for it.

(She tries to lunge again, but misses. **MAN** *and* **ICE TRAVELER** *exit. A red banner appears onstage and sweeps the area. The muffled sounds now become shouts of anger from the nation of* **MAN**. *Then the voices become silent.* **WOLF, PANDA BEAR,** *and* **SEA TURTLE** *enter. The sound of grass being whacked at is heard. The* **THREE** *see each other and sense it is wrong. They turn to exit, but* **MAN THREE** *and some other* **HUMANS** *enter.)*

MAN THREE. Get them! Don't be afraid! They are only animals. Tie them. Make sure you tie their binds tight. Hurry. Don't worry about the turtle. Work on the other two.

(The **MEN** *tie* **PANDA BEAR** *and* **WOLF**. *They place a muzzle on* **WOLF**. **SEA TURTLE** *has been placed on her back with a rock on her chest. The* **MEN** *exit.)*

We'll come back for them later.

WOLF. What do you think they will do to us?

SEA TURTLE. Oh – I don't want to think about it. I bet it will be bad.

WOLF. How do we get out?

SEA TURTLE. We are never going to get out.

PANDA BEAR. What is she... What are you doing, Wolf?

*(***WOLF** *is trying to howl as* **SEA TURTLE** *cries.)*

WOLF. Crying. And if I didn't have this thing on my mouth I could cry louder.

PANDA BEAR. Don't give up. Come on, you two. Please don't give up. We can get out of here. There is a possibility. Possibility leads to hope, hope leads to a solution.

(He struggles with the leash and ropes and breaks free, then he gets to his feet and stretches.)

PANDA BEAR. Ahh, that feels good.

(He pushes the rock off of **SEA TURTLE** *and turns her over, then he crosses over to* **WOLF** *and starts to chew on her muzzle.)*

WOLF. Ow! Watch where you're biting!

PANDA BEAR. Excuse me, but it blends so well with your color.

(They get the muzzle off and she is able to free herself. They get together in a small group.)

WOLF. Now what do we do?

PANDA BEAR. We'll sneak out together. Once we get some distance between the men, and us we'll try to find Ice Traveler. We will have Ice Traveler talk with Man. Maybe Man can talk with his people, hold a Council just for is nation. Hopefully we can have peace and restore the harmony we had.

WOLF. Then we must move quickly.

(They begin to leave and forget **SEA TURTLE.***)*

SEA TURTLE. Wait, wait. What about me? I can't keep up…

*(***PANDA BEAR** *and* **WOLF** *without hesitation return to help* **SEA TURTLE.** *They lift* **SEA TURTLE** *onto* **PANDA BEAR***'s back.)*

PANDA BEAR. Now, everyone – please be quiet.

(They sneak off. Blackout.)

Scene Eight

(MAN is trying to fish with no success. MAKO enters and makes a noise.)

MAN. Ice Traveler? Is that you? Ice Traveler?

(No response. MAKO makes a noise again.)

Ice Traveler? I've...

(MAKO swims around MAN, cutting off any escape.)

MAKO. Hellos, and smiles pretties for us. It is we, my little crunchy, munch. Smackities, smackities.

(MAN raises his harpoon.)

MAN. Get away from me!

MAKO. No, no – we no wants to get away from you. We wants to get closer to you, even better, so close, you be insides we forever. Yes, my little crunchies, munchies.

MAN. Get away! Leave me alone!

(MAN stabs at MAKO with the harpoon and then throws it at MAKO and misses.)

MAKO. Miss. He misses us, he really does. Now. We plays a game with it. Firsties, we goes out a little further. We needs more room to play. Yes, little man. Munchy, crunchies is ours. Yes it is. Now go.

(MAKO chases MAN out to sea.)

MAN. Help! Get away from me, Mako.

MAKO. Oh, what's wrong? We not wants to frightens, we wants crunchy munchies. Now swim faster, hurries, we wants to plays.

(*Goes underneath the water and nudges* **MAN**.)

MAN. Wait. Let's play a game.

MAKO. Smackity, smackities. We are-zees. We's playing, I am hungry, and you is crunchy, munchies.

MAN. No. Help me! Help!

ICE TRAVELER. (*Offstage.*) Leave him alone!

MAKO. No, no – it is her again.

(**ICE TRAVELER** *enters.*)

ICE TRAVELER. I've told you to keep away from him.

MAKO. We wills, we wills, for now. Don't bumps and bites us. Pretties and pleases.

(**MAKO** *begins to exit and stops.*)

We plays next time. You brings friends and we brings friends, we have feeding frenzies!

(**MAKO** *exits.*)

ICE TRAVELER. Get on my back, Man. There is something we have to do, and we don't have much time.

MAN. What are you talking about, ICE TRAVELER?

ICE TRAVELER. We are the only hope for the nations if there is going to be peace and harmony in this world. We can show the beings that there is a possibility of living together as one.

MAN. Those days are gone. I'm a Man and you're an animal. We'll never be equal again.

ICE TRAVELER. Do you really believe that, Man?

MAN. I – I don't know, Ice Traveler.

ICE TRAVELER. The world needs all the nations to live together in peace. We did it before. It's a knowledge that will never die but is sometimes forgotten. We have to make the people remember. Even if we have to bump and bit everyone. Look. We are closer to shore. See. There are people. They'll see us together, as one.

MAN. Ice Traveler, just you and I won't be enough to make them see that they're wrong.

>*(They are near shore, and **MAN** jumps off **ICE TRAVELER**.)*

I'll go to the shore from here, Ice Traveler. Alone.

>*(**MAN** beings to swim.)*

ICE TRAVELER. No, Man. Don't give up. What do I have to do to make all of you realize there is hope?

>*(She begins to swim to shore.)*

I am Ice Traveler of the Orca Nation. We can live together as one in the circle of life. The people of my nation will try to get on land and find those who are willing to work together as one. Live as one. Hear me, I am Ice Traveler...

>*(She beaches herself. **MAN** follows her.)*

MAN. Get back into the water, Ice Traveler. Please.

>*(**MAN** tries to move her.)*

Help me, Ice Traveler. I can't do this by myself. Please. Someone, anyone, we can't do this by ourselves. We need help from anyone who will give it. Please. I am Man, one of the nation of Man. We need your help.

>*(Blackout.)*

EPILOGUE

(Present day. **JOEY**, **MICHELLE**, *and the beached* **WHALES**.*)*

WHALE ONE. This is history.

WHALES TWO & THREE. Your history,

WHALES TOGETHER. Our history.

WHALE ONE. Can, can you,

WHALES TOGETHER. Help us?

MICHELLE. Yes. Um,

(She goes to the water, cups her hand, and brings water to the **WHALE**.*)*

Is it all right if I put water on you?

WHALE ONE. Thank you. It feels good, little one.

JOEY. Are you hurt really bad?

WHALE TWO. Wait. Can – can you tell us if things are continuing as they have been? We are looking for someone who will listen and help.

MICHELLE. Help? Our daddy is getting someone to help you now. Why – why are you here?

WHALE ONE. We are looking for someone who will sit and hold a council with us. Those who will listen and help. There are others from other nations in this world who are having a hard time, and they don't know how to ask for help.

MICHELLE. We'll do it. We'll hold council with you. We can help you. I am Michelle.

JOEY. I am Joey.

CHILDREN. We are from the nation of Man.

*(**FATHER** and another **MAN** enter. **MICHELLE** and **JOEY** cross to them and bring them near the **WHALES**. Blackout.)*

www.ingramcontent.com/pod-product-compliance
Lightning Source LLC
Chambersburg PA
CBHW072019290426
44109CB00018B/2293